I0559682

GROUP PORTRAIT:

Poems on a Photograph by Hermann Landshoff

MARK LUEBBERS & BENJAMIN GOLUBOFF

Copyright 2025 Mark Luebbers & Benjamin Goluboff
ISBN 978-1-957863-41-2

Cover Photo: "Artists in Exile"
    Sitter: Stanley William Hayter (1901 – 1988)
    Sitter: Leonora Carrington (1917 – 2011)
    Sitter: Frederick John Kiesler (1890 – 1965)
    Sitter: Kurt Seligmann (1900 – 1962)
    Sitter: Max Ernst (1891 – 1976)
    Sitter: Amedee Ozenfant (1886 – 1966)
    Sitter: Andre Breton (1896 – 1966)
    Sitter: Fernand Léger (1881 – 1955)
    Sitter: Berenice Abbott (1898 – 1991)
    Sitter: Jimmy Ernst (1920 – 1984)
    Sitter: Peggy Guggenheim (1898 – 1979)
    Sitter: John Ferren (1905 – 1970)
    Sitter: Marcel Duchamp (1887 – 1968)
    Sitter: Pieter Cornelis Mondrian (1872 – 1944)
    Artist: Hermann Landshoff (1905 – 1986)
    1942, Gelatin silver print
    National Portrait Gallery, Smithsonian Institution

    Used with permission of the National Portrait Gallery.

Published by Parisian Phoenix Publishing, Easton, Pennsylvania

CONNECT with the publisher:

 ParisianPhoenix

 ParisBirdBooks

 parisianphoenix

parisian phoenix
PUBLISHING

For Beth and for Catherine

Preface

The poems in this little volume explore Hermann Landshoff's photograph of modernist artists, most of them refugees from Hitler's Europe, gathered in the home of Peggy Guggenheim, patron and collector of modern art, in 1942. This group portrait is part of a series of photographs that Landshoff, himself a refugee, made of exiled artists and intellectuals in New York City during the war. The photograph may have been intended both as a statement of anti-fascist solidarity and as propaganda for Guggenheim's newly opened Art of This Century gallery. Landshoff appears to have made three closely related versions of the group portrait and given them the titles, variously, 'Artists in Exile' or 'The Surrealists.' The latter title is a misnomer because when Landshoff took the picture these artists were followers and leaders of several artistic movements including but not limited to Surrealism. The portrait is a rich visual text, an artifact of fourteen singular people who deeply influenced the arts and who also had complex relationships with each other.

The art historian Burcu Dogramaci reads the Landshoff photograph against Arthur Kaufmann's oil-on-canvas triptych group portrait "Arts and Science Finding Refuge in the U.S.A. — *Die geistige Emigration*, 1939–1964," whose thirty eight subjects include Einstein, Thomas Mann, and Paul Tillich. In ways that are not true or less true of the Kaufmann portrait, Dogramaci asserts, the Landshoff photo engages in playful subversion of the conventions of group portraiture inherited from the Dutch tradition, explores the working of human communities in ways compatible with Kurt Lewin's ideas on group dynamics, and offers, perhaps with tongue in cheek, an image of consensus. Dogramaci writes: "The photo leads to the impression that, beyond the real and conflict-ridden relationships between the protagonists, agreement and harmony seem to determine both the lives of the emigrants and those of their American colleagues" (9).

This is where we — poets never commended for our spirit of high seriousness — come in. We begin with the understanding that the agreement and harmony in the photograph are composed. We dwell upon the real and conflict-ridden relationships between the protagonists, even though we construe "real" broadly enough to

1

include various imaginary events. There is no record, for example, that Fernand Leger gazed upon the moon in the East River after being photographed, but we are pleased to imagine that he did. In the moment Landshoff took the picture, Amedee Ozenfant may not have been worrying about the rhyme between fascist ideologies and the party lines of the post-Cubist avant garde, but it suits our purposes to imagine it was so.

Nobody seems to have liked Peggy Guggenheim very much. Anton Gill, her most distinguished biographer, who tells her story with wise sympathy, presents Guggenheim as needy and grasping and heedless of the feelings of others. Mr. Gill joins the rest of us, however, in honoring the incomparable collection of art she built and left to the public (436). The Landshoff photograph is in dialogue with Guggenheim as collector and shares the joke that must have been on everybody's mind when the picture was taken — that Landshoff's subjects were like *objets* in a collection.

We have arranged the poems in an order that follows the artists' placement in the photograph: top row left to right, middle row left to right, bottom row likewise. A poem on Landshoff himself brings up the rear as a coda.

Also, we are aware that the Berenice Abbott poem reifies Queer desire through our collaborative cishet male gaze. We apologize. We could not help ourselves.

Finally, we thank The National Portrait Gallery of the Smithsonian Institution for their gracious permission to use the Landshoff photograph in our work.

WORKS CITED

Burcu Dogramaci, "Modern Group Portraits in New York Exile: Community and Belonging in the Work of Arthur Kaufmann and Hermann Landshoff" *Stedelijk Studies Journal 9* (2019).

Anton Gill, *Art Lover: A Biography of Peggy Guggenheim*. New York: Harper Collins, 2003.

Jimmy Ernst, Peggy Guggenheim, John Ferren, Marcel Duchamp, Piet Mondrian, Max Ernst, Amadee Ozenfant, Andre Breton, Fernand Leger, Berenice Abbott, Stanley Hayter, Leonora Carrington, Frederick Kiesler, Kurt Seligman

Photographer: Hermann Landshoff

Jimmy Ernst

It's always embarrassing when
more than one of Max's women is in the room,
embarrassing more for the elders than for Jimmy himself,
who is not only accustomed to these collisions
but capable of taking a certain pleasure
in the discomfort they cause everyone else.

Jimmy can feel it as the others arrange
themselves in rows before Landshoff's camera:
the *frisson* of a shared unspoken knowledge
provoking, variously, prurience and distaste.

Despite his short stature Jimmy is standing
in the back row next to Call-Me-Peggy
who is doing her best to look step-maternal
while staring kitchen knives at
Leonora Carrington who sits on the floor
between Stanley Hayter and Frederick Kiesler.

Out of the frame except when urgently,
calamitously at the center of the composition
for both father and son, Luise Strauss,
artist and critic, muse and memoirist,
Jimmy's mother, Max's first of many wives,
is with considerable dignity going down to darkness
first at Camp de Gurs, then Drancy, then at Auschwitz.

Max has escaped Europe only a month earlier,
through Lisbon and on the wings,
as it seems to everyone,
of Call-me-Peggy, but it was Jimmy
(arrived two years ago, a kid,
twenty, a brand from the burning)
whose letters to the Emergency Relief Committee
had gotten Max his visa.

And Jimmy is thinking that it feels like Europe
with Max and the oldsters forming up
in the tall-ceilinged foyer
of Peggy's grandiose house on the East River.
Kiesler, that poisonous little gnome,
is the only German beside Max,
but all the elder Frogs, *les eminences*,
make it reminiscent for Jimmy
of childhood visits to Max
at Nice or Juan Les Pins
where one or another French colleague
or mistress or hanger-on would rain down
Gallic *politesse* upon the little boy.

And they are all good fun, Max's oldsters:
the *bonhomie*, the *savoir faire*, the *aperçus*
— boy do they have *aperçus*!
But Jimmy feels not at all identified with the old guys.
In ways of which he is only partly cognizant
the young painter feels like more of an American
than the other artists in the photograph.
His youth is part of the equation here.
Also his two years, pre-Peggy, of making
his way in Manhattan.
Maybe Jimmy discerns in the sprawl,
the ambition, the fatherlessness of the young nation,
some resemblance to himself.

Besides:

What's Europe when there's a guy
in Washington Square Park flying a parrot on a tether,
when Chinatown is open all night?
What's Europe when Earl Hines
leads the house band at the Savoy,
when Motherwell is just back from Mexico
with a suitcase full of light?
What's Europe when Luise
is about to go up the chimney?

It may be that Jimmy hears
the hinge of history creaking,
that he feels the plates about to shift.
Perhaps he is aware that he is breathing
the rare high air near the summit
of the American Century.

The young painter wears
a startled expression in the photograph
because in the instant that the shutter snaps
Peggy pinches Jimmy's ass.

Peggy Guggenheim

Get out of my house,
Leonora Carrington.
Get out of my house.

John Ferren

At his easel in the garden, the artist was approached by an acquaintance who asked, "Are you painting the garden?" He replied, "I am not."

The artist's friend visited his studio and asked the name of a particular shade in one of his paintings. The artist was silent and pointed to the door.

A student asked the artist how he should paint the first stroke on a new canvas. The artist said, "Drink a glass of water."

Seated beside him on a bench one afternoon, a scholar asked the artist for his theory of composition. After a silence the artist asked, "Does a mountain create space or consume it?"

Another student asked how to paint the perfect form of a delicate vase. The artist picked up the vase and dropped it to the floor.

Alone at work, late at night, the artist struggled not to paint a shape onto the canvas before him. After a long period of concentration, he succeeded.

The artist was poor and had only enough paint for one composition, but he made three: one using the paint, another using the idea of the paint, and one using neither paint nor ideas.

Asked about the meaning of symbols in his work, the artist explained "These symbols transcend symbols, and therefore mean nothing."

An aspirant begged the artist to show him the proper positioning of brush and hand before the canvas. Just then a bird alighted in a tree outside the window. The aspirant bowed.

Piet Mondrian

stood in the back row beside Duchamp
turned his left shoulder dutifully to the camera
like the others, and considered age:

its plastic effect
on one's ideals, how
it multiplies and alloys
the once-pure foundation
of principle, how the reach
past objects for the absolute
becomes longer, then requires
supplement and compromise
how, if one is not fully aware
the hard lines that separate
necessity from conviction
can at first become thin
then bend, and finally
vanish altogether.

Marcel Duchamp

Chess became so absorbing for
Marcel that eventually he allowed
it into his carefully managed version
of reality. At a party perhaps, or on

a train, he would read the space and
its occupants, casting each person
as a chess piece based on what
he knew of their character and

relation to the others present. If
some persons were unknown to the
artist, reducing each to a type would
reveal for Duchamp their role and

place on the board. This stern
old man: a bishop, this flirtatious
young woman: a rook. All the brave
and hapless pawns inching along to

doom. And he played both sides
of course. With concentration and
practice he was able to move the
pieces according to his will; discern,

predict, and execute their behavior.
A laugh or petty insult, a false look
of desire, a foolish boast or retreat
from conversation. Marcel could see

these coming and force, block, or
pass the pieces as he chose. Better
even than chess with inanimate
pieces, Duchamp's invention was

not subject to the static laws of a
match. No gambit was impossible,
nor was there objective victory or
defeat, and each game was, in theory

at least, endless. Here in front of
Landshoff's camera, however,
Duchamp had found the limit of
his skills. This was a set he could

not analyze, let alone manipulate.
Mme. G. — queen of course, but in
this formation, was Max a knight
en prise or merely a poisoned pawn?

And what of Ozenfant: trapped
or forced? King Andre — under
battery? Did Leonora hold the
initiative? Perhaps he knew these
colleagues too well to advance them
by tactic and position, or perhaps he
could not know them well enough.
This thought made him uneasy, but
there was another that terrified
him: maybe he was just a piece on
the board, not the player, and this
was the cause of his helplessness.

Max Ernst

Often he had spoken of collage
as systematic displacement:
the fracturing of what was coherent
and the arrangement of the disjointed
pieces into a counter-statement.

Perhaps then he had become
another composition of his making:
Herr Bricolage, Die Anatomie
a puppet made of fragments
an assemblage of contradictions.

So that seated now in front
of his benefactor and betrothed
he sensed his reconstructed image
posing a question to the camera.

Something about money
as the essential medium
for both artist and charlatan
and whether it can make one
into the other.

Amédée Ozenfant

After the last war, it had seemed imperative to dispel chaos from art, to bring sense into the business of perception, to make a new design for living. Doing so, he believed, would require the organizing mechanisms of the eye and the mind to erase the fragmentary, the misleading, and the vague.

So he had proposed a new aesthetic: an art based on clarity and resolution. Paintings of useful objects arranged with beautiful logic, their presence perfected, unencumbered by decoration or distraction, and colored gently, if at all. This was vision at once concentrated and made pure.

Over time, through the writing and teaching of these precepts, he had found some measure of success, though perhaps not like those Dada provocateurs, or the Abstracts with all their drama. Nonetheless, the passing years had made him comfortable, highly-regarded, and he was known for being sure of what he was known for.

But now the rationale of purity had been deployed by entire nations in the service of a new war, one which was at once eating and vomiting the world whole, and thus he had arrived at what one might call a reassessment, if not doubt or regret, regarding his tenured and beloved doctrine.

And he could not keep himself from the proposition that to ignore the strings of a violin or the dust on a bottle, to reject the cracks in a vase, to eliminate unsightly variation and difference, to seek always a reduction of what one decides to see, is not the resolution of underlying truth, but rather the abnegation of its wholeness, and that such a practice is in effect the taking off, rather than the putting on, of one's spectacles.

Andre Breton

The world changed for Andre, very suddenly, in '37,
or maybe it was '38,
in Mexico City, the Coyoacan District,
when he first had *mole*.

In Coyoacan it's all the time up for grabs:
kids in the fountains, pet anacondas,
madmen climbing the streetlight poles,
fireworks launched from Parish Bautista.
And there in some homely *cantina*
— El Potosi it was called —
Andre had the *pollo en mole*
and it spun his cap.

The Coyoacan mole made '37,
or maybe '38, Year Zero for Andre.
Here Alpha kissed Omega.
Praxis assisted Theoria in auto-erotic asphyxiation.
Dark emissaries from the blood bore gifts of wisdom to the mind
and were rebuffed with theatrical gestures of derision.
Mythic coyotes consorted with the god of flowers.

Even allowing for a certain Eurocentric exoticism on poor Andre's part,
this was some ooey-gooey icky-sticky D.H.Lawrence
kind of shit he was into here
and he could not get enough.
Mole was surreal.

Andre loved New York when he got there in '42,
called it Babylon on the Hudson.
His one complaint about the city: no place to get *mole*.

Fernand Leger

His face is creased and totemic,
the corners of his mouth turn downwards.

He is thinking that capitalism is both
productive of and dependent on crisis,

that it renews its capacity to exploit labor
and accumulate value as crises of supply

or crises of valuation reshape the means
or the relations of production.

After being photographed Leger
will gaze upon the moon in the East River.

Berenice Abbott

Oh Leonora, we shall
all the pleasures prove.
All of them. We shall.

And time, Leonora!
We should make much of it.
The virgins, the rosebuds!

Mark but this flea, Leonora.
Country matters!
Country matters!

I will be your wife, Leonora,
if you will marry me.
If not, I'll die your maid.

Stanley Hayter

1.
With
        the onset
        of hostilities
the Home Guard
        enlisted his
                help
        in the
    development
of new
        forms and
                techniques
of
camouflage.

At first
        it seemed
                a contradiction
for
a printmaker
        but
    he found   himself
        after   taking
the job merely
        as his bit
                for king
                        and country
            to be
absorbed
        by
        the design
        of   diffusion
                the artistry
    of apparent   absence
in making
                the extant
                    appear   to disappear
                        so as to
                    conjure
                    the opposite
                            of image.

18

2.
Now transplanted
          by his   patroness
and installed
                    safely
                         at The New
               School
he was
          reprising his role
               as
          L'enseignant Célèbre´
     oracle   of intaglio
     master   of the burin
               with earnest young
                              Yanks
          this time coming
to sit beside
               his aura.

He was
not
          at all
                    ungrateful
it was
good to have
                    the work
                         and
          he made
                    the most
          of the
          performance
                    played   kind Socrates
                    gave   forth
all
   the wisdom
               he could
                         conjure.

But
        at times   like this
            posed before
           a camera
               with others
        of the flock
he felt   exposed
           too   visible
        and imagined
        ways
           to shroud himself
behind
a
        graphic of
              illegibility
        one which would
        allow him
to be   present   but secreted
              behind
                good
cover.

Leonora Carrington

At the bottom of the garden there are ghosts of several kinds.
These include varieties of horse ghosts: the local Shire,
extinct North American, Arabian, and Rocking.

Also present are ghosts of the dispossessed:
local hands and the starved children of local hands,
the slaves Enclosure made.

In this pale darkness at the bottom of the garden
it is possible to figure lines of commerce
between the horses and the ghosts
to see them as together involved in a direction
or tendency orientated to the upper right.

There is an open window here and through it one sees
that the ghost of the extinct North American horse
feels sympathy for the ghosts of the dispossessed,
considers extinction to be a form of Enclosure,
a banning from the Earth.

Also present are the ghosts of usages and traditions
that died when our woods were enclosed:
rights of way and rights of forage, rights to firewood,
to summer's berries, whortle and goose,
to fatten pigs on the mast of the elder oaks.

Between darkness and moon-shadow,
making a focal point for the direction or tendency
orientated to the upper right, the ghost of Captain Pouch,
proletarian rebel, rides a rocking horse
through our enclosed woods.

Frederick Kiesler

was bemused, and turned to Leonora
when she said;
"Our spirits live inside the walls
of our bodies, just as our bodies
live inside the walls of our homes."

For a moment he took this as
one of her fine absurdities
but then the words made him wonder
if spaces can live with us inside
like organs, with walls like skin
a single organism
made of home and occupant
a structure made as much
of flesh and sensibility
as wood and stone and glass.

From his place on the floor
he scanned the room:
a collection of artifacts
idols, *objets moderne*, and now
this array of refugees.
A place composed, it seemed
as a stage
in the theater of assets
or a shop window
at the ego boutique.

The observation brought to him
a second possibility, and he replied
though he was not sure she heard
"Perhaps one can either be sustained
or consumed by where one lives."

Kurt Seligman

1.
would die in 1962
when he slipped down
the icy front stoop
of his farmhouse upstate,
and the shotgun
he was carrying
went off in his hands.

He was taking it
within range
of his birdfeeder
where he liked
to shoot the rodents
stealing the seed.

2.
as he painted, saw in his mind the old pageants
held in Basel when he was a boy.
The *Danses Macabre* celebrating Carnival Day
when, in arcane headgear and costumes
the knights and hunters of legend
brandished their mock weaponry
and revelers flailed and wheeled in time
to the concussion of the city's great drums
catching him again in the absurd parade.

Hermann Landshoff

All the celebrity in the room was like a gas
making him slightly ill
and prompting in the photographer the old feeling
that he was an imposter in his vocation:
Herr Landshoff the jobber, the stringer who does weddings
bar mitzvahs, and fashion shoots
who does not do the real thing.
It was hard to call himself an artist with Leger looking back at him.

But like many real artists in various media, Landshoff was a collector
driven by an appetite to gather, control, and possess his subjects
first by arranging them before the exposure
then through manipulations of them in the darkroom.
And owning the image, keeping or selling as he chose
was sometimes a greater satisfaction than making the photograph.
These records of his gaze were a way of laying claim.

So when it turned out the Surrealists had devised
their own pose to mock the American press
which treated them as a unit, a dance band, or a football team
he saw them making off with a rightful asset.
And this was why in the seconds after he took the *Official* portrait
just as the artists were breaking ranks
Landshoff squeezed the trigger again, then a time or two again
just to make sure he had them all.

About the Authors

Mark Luebbers lives and writes in Princeton, Massachusetts. His poems have appeared in journals including *The American Journal of Poetry*, *The Museum of Americana*, *Apple Valley Review*, *Blue Line*, *The Hopper*, *Salt Front*, *The Wayfarer Magazine*, and *Wilderness House Review*. His collection *Flat Light* was published by Urban Farmhouse Press in 2020.

Benjamin Goluboff teaches at Lake Forest College. In addition to some scholarly publications, he has placed imaginative writing — poetry, fiction, and essays — in many small-press journals, including *Hayden's Ferry Review*, *South Dakota Review*, and *War Literature and the Arts*. He is the author of *Ho Chi Minh: A Speculative Life in Verse* and *Biking Englewood: An Essay on the White Gaze*, both from Urban Farmhouse Press. Ben's collection, *Moe Asch: A Speculative Life in Verse* is forthcoming from Kelsay Press.

Mark and Ben have collaborated on speculative biographical poetry since the middle of the last decade. Poems they've written together have appeared in many small-press journals including *Misfit Magazine*, *Paper Brigade*, and *The Penn Review*. In 2018 three of their poems on jazz pianist Bill Evans were collected in *They Said: A Multi Genre Anthology of Contemporary Collaborative Writing*, from Black Lawrence Press. Their collection *Citizens of Ordinary Time*, appeared from Urban Farmhouse Press in 2023.

COLOPHON:

The sans serif typeface used in this chapbook is Neue Kabel. It was designed for metal type in 1927 by German type designer Rudolf Koch (1876–1934). The "neue" digital edition version was revived and restored in 2013 by Marc Schütz. It is simple, clean, and classic with a hint of the Bauhaus aesthetic.

www.ingramcontent.com/pod-product-compliance
Lightning Source LLC
Chambersburg PA
CBHW051252120626
46547CB00014B/1919